Food from Farmers

MILK!

Life on a Dairy Farm

by Ruth Owen

WINDMILL BOOKS

New York

Published in 2012 by Windmill Books, an Imprint of Rosen Publishing
29 East 21st Street, New York, NY 10010

Editor for Ruby Tuesday Books Ltd: Mark J. Sachner
U.S. Editor: Julia Quinlan
Designer: Emma Randall
Consultant: Logan Peterman, Laughing Sprout Family Farm

Cover, 1, 4–5, 6–7, 8–9, 10–11, 12–13, 14–15, 16–17, 18, 19 (bottom), 20 (top left), 20 (top right), 21, 22, 23 (bottom), 24–25, 26–27, 28–29, 30–31 © Shutterstock; 19 (top) © FLPA; 23 (top) © Wikipedia (Creative Commons public domain) Gary D. Robson.

Library of Congress Cataloging-in-Publication Data

Owen, Ruth, 1967–
 Milk! : life on a dairy farm / by Ruth Owen.
 p. cm. — (Food from farmers)
 Includes index.
 ISBN 978-1-61533-528-2 (library binding) — ISBN 978-1-61533-534-3 (pbk.) —
ISBN 978-1-61533-535-0 (6-pack)
 1. Milk—Juvenile literature. 2. Dairy processing—Juvenile literature. 3. Dairy cattle—
Juvenile literature. I. Title.
SF251.O94 2012
637—dc23
                              2011022783

Manufactured in the United States of America

CPSIA Compliance Information: Batch #BOW2102WM: For Further Information contact Windmill Books, New York, New York at 1-866-478-0556

CONTENTS

WELCOME TO MY FARM!

Hi! My name is Michael. I am eleven years old. I live on a farm with my dad and my sister. Our farm is a dairy farm.

A dairy farm is a farm where milk is produced. The milk we produce comes from dairy cows.

Dairy farm

Our farm is an **organic farm**. This means we produce milk in a way that is kind to planet Earth! I will tell you more about being organic later in the book.

Dairy cows

We give every cow on the farm a name. This is Lillie. She is nine years old. Lillie is my favorite cow on the farm.

LILLIE'S FARM FACTS

- There are over 55,000 dairy farms in the United States.
- There are nearly 13,000 dairy farms in Canada.
- Some dairy farms produce milk from goats or sheep.

LET'S LOOK AROUND THE FARM

This is a map of our farm. We live in the farmhouse.

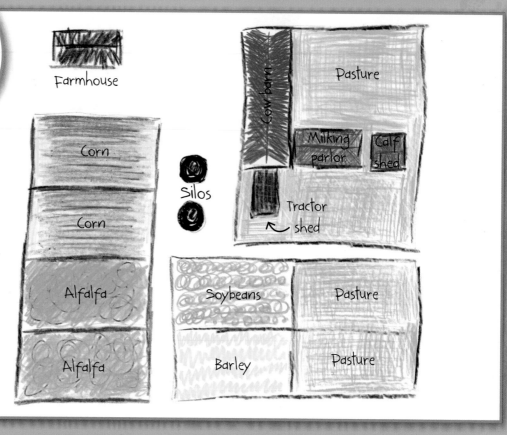

Farmhouse

Corn

Corn

Alfalfa

Alfalfa

Silos

Cow barn

Pasture

Milking parlor

Calf shed

Tractor shed

Soybeans

Pasture

Barley

Pasture

Let's take a look around the farm!

This is the **pasture**. The cows live here in the summer.

In the winter, the cows live in the barn.

Pasture

Barn

We grow **crops** for the cows to eat.
We grow corn, alfalfa, barley, and soybeans.

Alfalfa field

Cornfield

Barley field

Soybean field

This is Dad with the soybean crop.

The farm used to belong to my grandpa. Dad took over the farm when my grandpa died. I want to take over the farm when I grow up!

LILLIE'S FARM FACTS

- In the United States, 99 out of 100 dairy farms are owned and run by just one family.

MEET THE COWS

The dairy cows live in a big group called a herd.

There are 250 milking cows and 25 **heifers** in our herd. A heifer is a young female cow. The heifers will become milking cows when they grow up.

Heifer

Milking Cow

Every cow is given a number when it is born.
The cow's number is shown on its ear tag.
The number allows the farmer to keep a record
of the cow for its whole life.
The record keeps track of when the cow was born.
It may also show whether the cow has been ill.

Ear Tag

The cows on our farm are Holstein cows.

LILLIE'S COOL COW FACTS

- **Most Holstein cows are black and white. Some are brownish-red and white.**

- **Every Holstein cow has a different pattern.**

9

WHAT DO COWS EAT?

Cows eat grass. Lots of grass!
In the summer, they live in the pasture.
They eat grass all day long.

LILLIE'S COOL COW FACTS

- A dairy cow needs to eat up to 100 pounds (45 kg) of food each day. It also drinks enough water to fill a bathtub!

In the fall and winter, the grass doesn't grow.
We have to feed the cows eight meals every day!

We feed the cows dried grass called hay.
We make hay from alfalfa.

We also feed the cows a special mixture of foods
such as barley, soybeans, and corn.
The special mixture is called total mixed rations.

Total mixed rations are like a complete cow dinner!

Total mixed rations

LET'S LOOK INSIDE A COW!

This might sound a bit yucky, but cows have a really amazing stomach! A cow's stomach has four different compartments.

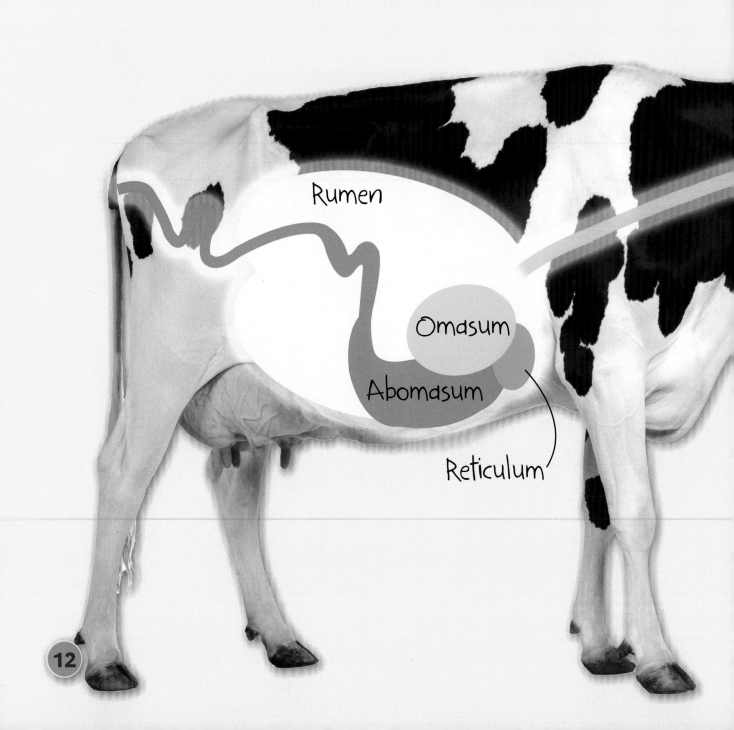

Rumen

Omasum

Abomasum

Reticulum

LILLIE'S COOL COW FACTS

- **A cow will spend up to 10 hours each day chewing the cud.**

- A cow chews up grass and swallows it.

- The grass goes into the rumen. Here, stomach juices start to soften the grass.

- Next, the grass goes into the reticulum. The grass is turned into balls of grass, called cuds.

- The cuds go back up into the cow's mouth. The cow chews the cuds.

- The cuds are swallowed and go into the omasum.

- Finally, the food moves into the abomasum. Here, the cow's body takes **nutrients** from the food.

Nutrients are all the good things that a body needs to keep working.

13

HOW DO COWS MAKE MILK?

When a cow is ready to have a baby, her body starts producing milk.

A baby cow is called a calf.

To make milk, the cow's body takes water and nutrients from her blood. Then it turns them into milk.
The milk is stored in the cow's udder.
The milk comes out of the cow's four teats.

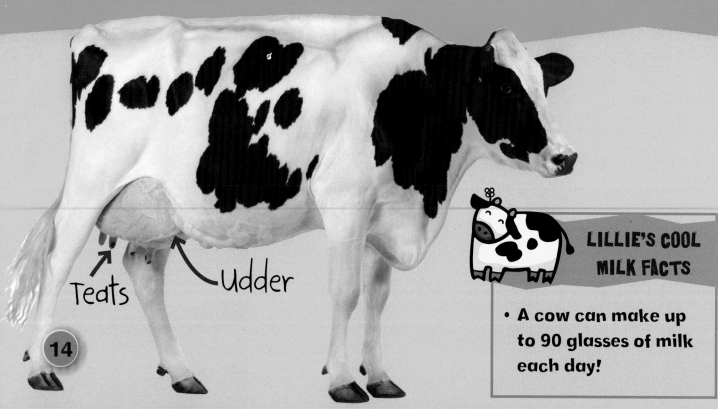

Teats

Udder

LILLIE'S COOL MILK FACTS

- A cow can make up to 90 glasses of milk each day!

When one of our cows gives birth, Dad tries to be close by.
He wants to make sure the cow and calf are well.
The cows can give birth to their calves at any time.
Sometimes Dad has to go to a birth in the middle of the night!

CARING FOR THE CALVES

A calf spends its first day with its mother. Then it goes to live in the calf shed with lots of other calves.

Right now, we have 20 calves on our farm. We feed the calves with big bottles of milk.

I help Dad feed the calves in the morning before I go to school.

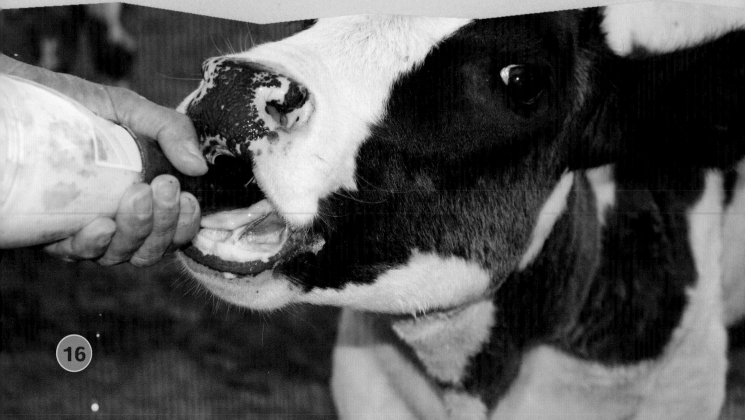

As the calves grow bigger, we feed them hay and other foods to help them grow.

The female calves will become dairy cows when they grow up. We sell the male calves to a beef farm. They are raised for meat.

LILLIE'S COOL COW FACTS

- A Holstein calf can weigh 90 pounds (41 kg) when it is born.
- An adult Holstein cow can weigh 1,500 pounds (680 kg).

IT'S TIME TO MILK THE COWS!

We milk the cows in the **milking parlor**. They are milked in the morning and in the afternoon.

The cows wait at the pasture gate when it is time to be milked.

18

The milking machine is attached to the cow's teats.
The machine squeezes to make the milk come out.
When the cow's udder is empty, the machine stops.

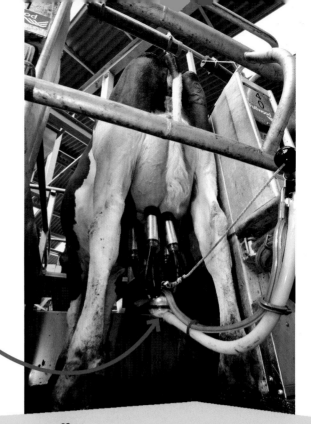

Milking machine

The cow's milk is warm. It flows into a big tank through pipes that cool it down.

LILLIE'S COOL MILK FACTS

- **The milk is never touched by a person. It's all done by machines!**

Soon, the tanker truck arrives to collect the milk.
The driver tests the milk to make sure it is healthy and germ-free.
Then, the milk is pumped into the tanker, and it's off to the **dairy plant.**
The workers at the plant will get the milk ready for people to drink.

Tanker truck

A DAY IN THE LIFE OF A FARM

Dairy farmers work very hard!
Here is what a day
on our farm is like.

1:00 a.m.
Dad goes to the barn to check on a calf
that has just been born.

Annie and her
husband Bob
work on the
farm with Dad.

4:00 a.m.
Dad and Annie start the milking.

7:00 a.m.
Milking is finished, so it's time
to clean the milking parlor.

8:00 a.m.
Dad and I feed the calves.

11:00 a.m.
When the cows are living in the barn it must be cleaned every day. The walkways are washed and the cows get clean bedding.

LILLIE'S COOL COW FACTS

- **Farmers use straw, wood chips, shredded-up rubber, and even beach sand for cow bedding.**

3:00 p.m.
It's time to milk the cows for the second time.

Time for a drink of milk!

7:00 p.m.
Dad cooks supper for my sister Ellie and me.

ALWAYS BUSY ON THE FARM

Dad doesn't just care for the cows.
There are lots of other jobs to be done on a dairy farm!

Tractor

Plow

In the spring, Dad plants our crops.
The plow digs up the soil so it is ready for the seeds.

When the corn is fully grown,
we harvest it to make **silage**.
The corn is chopped into small
pieces and put into the **silos**.
The corn turns into soft, sugary
silage for the cows to eat.

Silo

Hay bale

Dad cuts the alfalfa and dries it in the sun to make hay. A machine makes the hay into big bundles called bales. The cows will eat the hay during the winter.

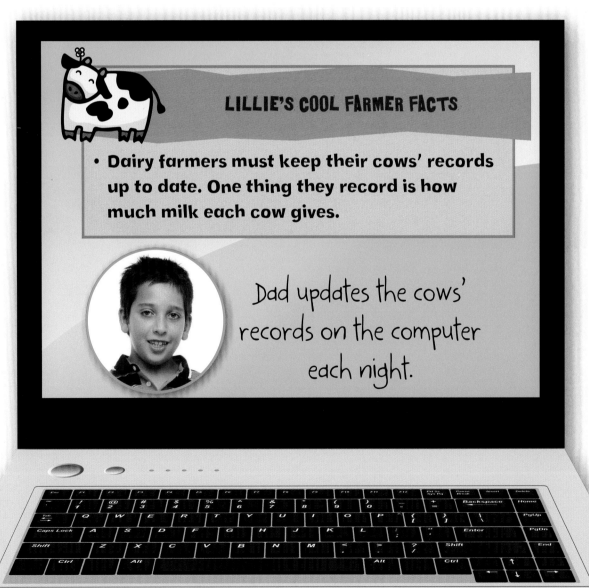

LILLIE'S COOL FARMER FACTS

- Dairy farmers must keep their cows' records up to date. One thing they record is how much milk each cow gives.

Dad updates the cows' records on the computer each night.

LIFE ON AN ORGANIC DAIRY FARM

We do all we can to be kind to animals and take care of the planet.

Many dairy cows spend all their lives in a barn. That's too bad, because cows like to eat grass and be outside in the fresh air.
On an organic dairy farm, like ours, the cows spend time outside, in a pasture.

Many farms cut down trees to make bigger fields.
Dad has planted lots of trees on our farm. They give birds, insects, and wild animals a place to live.

24

We use a machine called a digester to turn cow **manure** into energy. The digester uses the gases from the manure to make all the electricity our farm needs!

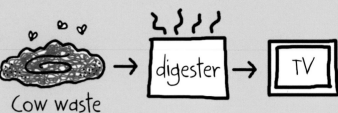

Cow waste   →   digester   →   TV

LILLIE'S COOL ORGANIC FACTS

- Some farms use chemicals to help their crops grow. Chemical plant foods are made in factories that use lots of energy. Organic dairy farms use manure from their cows to feed the crops.

Recycling cow waste as plant food is cool!

AT THE DAIRY PLANT

The milk from our farm goes to an organic dairy plant. Hundreds of organic dairy farms send their milk here every day.

Dairy plant

At the plant the milk is **pasteurized**. Pasteurization kills off any germs that could make a person sick. The milk is heated to 161 degrees Fahrenheit (72 degrees Celsius) for 15 seconds. Then it is quickly cooled down.

At the plant, the milk is put into bottles and cartons.

The milk is also made into **dairy foods** such as cheese, cream, yogurt, and butter.

This milk is being made into cheese.

The dairy plant sells the milk and dairy foods to supermarkets and grocery stores.

LILLIE'S COOL MILK FACTS

• **Always keep milk in the refrigerator.**

• **Close up the container after you pour it.**

• **Buy milk last at the store so it doesn't get too warm while you look around.**

WE LOVE MILK!

Milk tastes great, and it's filled with good stuff that your body needs.

Milk contains **calcium**, which helps make your bones and teeth strong. Milk also contains **Vitamin** D. This vitamin helps your body use calcium.

Milk contains **protein** for building muscles. It keeps your muscles healthy and strong, too. Milk also gives you energy!

These are my favorite ways to get my milk nutrients.

I eat cereal for breakfast with lots of icy cold milk.

Ellie and I make our own flavored milk. Chocolate milk is my favorite!

Dad sprinkles extra cheese on my pizza.

LILLIE'S COOL MILK TIPS

- **Stay fit and healthy by having low-fat milk or dairy foods, such as cheese and yogurt, three times every day.**

Thank you to dairy farmers and dairy cows everywhere!

GLOSSARY

calcium (KAL-see-um)
A nutrient needed for strong bones and teeth. It is found in dairy foods.

crops (KRAHPS)
Plants that are grown in large quantities on a farm.

dairy foods (DER-ee FOODZ)
Foods made from milk, such as cheese, butter, cream, and yogurt.

dairy plant (DER-ee PLANT)
A factory where milk is pasteurized and packaged. Dairy foods are sometimes made here, too.

heifer (HEH-fur)
A young female cow that has not yet had a calf.

manure (muh-NOOR)
Animal waste.

milking parlor (MILK-ing PAR-lur)
A building on a dairy farm where cows go to be milked by milking machines.

nutrients (NOO-tree-ents)
Substances that the body needs to help it live and grow. Foods

contain nutrients such as vitamins and protein.

organic farm (or-GA-nik FARM)
A farm that doesn't use chemicals to feed crops or kill insect pests and weeds. Organic farms also let animals live a more natural life outside instead of keeping them in barns. These farms are kinder to animals and help keep the planet healthy.

pasteurized (PAS-chuh-ryzd)
Heated to a high temperature and then cooled to kill germs.

pasture (PAS-chur)
A field where livestock, such as cows or sheep, can eat grass.

protein (PROH-teen)
A nutrient needed by the body. It is found in foods such as milk, meat, and fish.

silage (SY-lij)
Animal feed made from plants that have been softened in a silo.

silo (SY-loh)
A large metal container, often like a tower, used for storing grain on a farm or for making silage.

vitamin (VY-tuh-min)
A substance found in foods that is needed by the body for health and growth.

WEB SITES
For Web resources related to the subject of this book, go to: www.windmillbooks.com/weblinks and select this book's title.

READ MORE

Gibbons, Gail. *The Milk Makers.* New York: Aladdin, 1987.

Pohl, Kathleen. *What Happens at a Dairy Farm? (Where People Work).* New York: Weekly Reader Early Learning, 2006.

Mercer, Abbie. *Cows on a Farm.* New York: PowerKids Press, 2009.

INDEX